Manufactured by Amazon.ca
Bolton, ON

23058647R00068